BRISTOL ON OLD POSTCARDS

Volume Three

Compiled by

Janet and Derek Fisher
Mildred and Francis Ford
(founder members of Bristol Postcard Club)

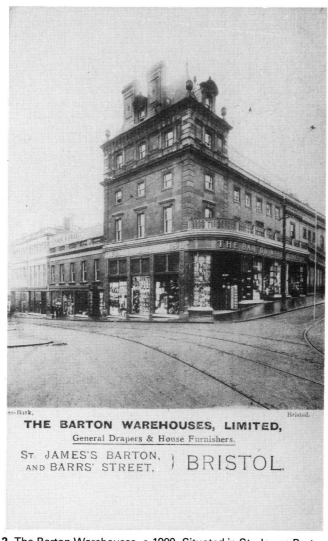

2. The Barton Warehouses, c.1900. Situated in St. James Barton, this fine building was a casualty of the blitz. Barr Street, which was situated to the left, was closed and new stores were opened in 1957. The postcard was used by the firm as an advertising card.

£3.95

**Designed and Published by
Reflections of a Bygone Age,
Keyworth, Nottingham.
1987**

ISBN 0 946245 19 3

3. Peter Street, c.1890. Church Lane connected Peter Street with Narrow Wine Street. Mrs. Kealings, the apple woman, was a familiar figure on this corner, and used to live in the courtyard in Tower Street. The notice board on the wall advises cyclists to *"stop here for good accommodation"*. Footwear in profusion hangs outside the corner shop. Are the boys waiting for a free apple? Photographic card with no publisher indicated.

**Printed by
Adlard Print and Typesetting Services,
Ruddington, Notts.**

INDEX

Cover Pictures:

Front: Victoria and Temple Streets, Bristol, on an Edwardian postcard published by Hartmann.

Back: (top left) Bristol heraldic card, posted in the city in October 1907.

(top right) Advertising card drawn by John Hassall, who designed many comic picture postcards. The picture was probably used by many firms for publicity - in this instance by Parrish's of Park Row.

(bottom) The card was probably published about 1910, though the scene is the Dutch House, Bristol, in 1878. Published by J. Salmon of Sevenoaks, and painted by E. A. Phipson.

Picture Postcards were not introduced in Britain until 1894, though they had been popular on the Continent for over 20 years. The early British cards were known as Court Cards (size 115 x 89 mm), smaller than the Continental size of 140 x 89 mm, and the message had to be written on the same side as the picture, leaving the back for the stamp and address. This obviously inhibited the possibilities for illustrations, so when the Post Office permitted the use of the larger-size card (1899) and the 'divided back' (1902) where message and address occupied the same side, the publishers were able to exploit the postcard much more effectively, and a flood of cards on every imaginable subject was produced.

The postcard fulfilled several functions: it was a medium for communicating simple messages and greetings (mail was reliably delivered within 24 hours, and over short distances, on the same day). Firms used them as advertising material and correspondence cards. Photographs of special events and disasters provided a unique pictorial record of local happenings. Comic postcards gave people the opportunity to send risqué messages to their friends. Soon, the collecting of all these cards became a major hobby, and the reign of Edward VII paralleled the 'golden age' of Picture Postcards, with many thousands of families amassing vast numbers sent from all over Britain (and, for those with wealthy connections, the Continent). Specialist magazines catered for the craze, and publishers produced cards on all kinds of themes: railways, actresses, military, shipping, glamour, children, heraldic, royalty, political - as well as greetings, comic cards and street scenes. The Great War saw new themes developed - patriotic, political satire, and beautiful silk cards, embroidered in France, and sent home by British tommies to be lovingly treasured. Postcard collecting ceased to have the same meaning and appeal after the war, though. The quality of production deteriorated (some of the best pre-1914 cards had been printed in Germany), the postage rate doubled, and the national mood and social conditions had changed out of all recognition: it was a new era, with changed values and priorities. 'Golden Age' postcards lay neglected in their albums in attics for years, until a few enthusiasts in the 1950's ushered a new-found appreciation for the beautiful old cards to a whole new generation. Their availability, though, remained confined to the shelves of occasional book and antique shops, and new-wave collectors didn't find it easy to build up collections. All that changed in the 1970's. A travelling exhibition organised by the Victoria and Albert Museum, the emergence of specialist dealers, magazines, catalogues and fairs, had the effect of encouraging a host of new collectors and a consequent upsurge in prices. By then, Edwardian albums were emerging from the attics, as their original owners or their sons and daughters died. Now, the hobby is thriving, and the beautiful postcard issues of the Edwardian era are once again lovingly collected.

INTRODUCTION   by Rosemary Clinch

Every picture is worth a thousand words, but none can tell stories more vividly than old picture postcards. They are like a window on the past reflecting the life of the day, a fixed point in time recorded by a postmark and a brief personal message. To study them is to summon back an age which for some holds a deep sense of nostalgia, a yearning for the past, feelings which grow more precious as the years go by. It is these things which give them a special quality, an added dimension to a delightful historical record.

There is a thriving passion for collecting old picture postcards and nowhere more than in Bristol as their popularity increases. My own enthusiasm came through a desire to illustrate the books I write. While my camera can achieve mostly what I seek, it is often the old picture postcard which completes the story, allowing the reader a visual journey into the past. I, like others, am tempted to search the attic of my ancestors in the hope of finding a dusty old album rich with 'pickings' from the past. I join the bowed heads in antique shops and markets, second-hand dealers and postcard fairs, where hands work feverishly through cardboard boxes. The joy of finding another card for a set or for illustration is immeasurable, while a message read can be intriguing. *'Dear C - Very griefed to hear from Ethel that you are giving so much trouble.'* Maybe someone from Essex had deserved a well-earned rest while on holiday in Bristol in 1907!

Bristol, fortunate in her history, saw publishers produce familiar studies of the city's heritage which was destined to see many changes and developments. Local photographers explored the city and the growing urban areas, expertly capturing in black and white, typical street scenes, the architecture, the curious onlooker and inhabitants from all walks of Edwardian life. Firms produced postcards for promoting their products. Comic cards induced an element of fun between friends while special events of local happenings provided a unique record.

As the older generation passes, new cards by local photographers are found and it is these which are the most valuable. Reproductions of Victorian photographs by Fred Little are rare but those mostly sought by local collectors are the Edwardian scenes of Bristol by people like Garrett. My own collection being modest, I often enlist the help of the Bristol Postcard Club's founder-members for illustrations more difficult to obtain. Their love and appreciation of Bristol's heritage is an inspiration for the need for research into what is a valuable addition to a city's historical record. I value the help they have given me and the opportunity of being able to share in the fruits of their dedicated work by collecting their books of *Bristol on Old Postcards*. I welcome this, their third volume, for their continuing enthusiasm makes it possible for *all* to enjoy a journey into a great city's past - a visual treat and a lasting pleasure.

Rosemary Clinch is a prolific author, with her two best-known local titles being 'Unknown Bristol' and 'Curious Bristol'.

5. THE OLD DRAWBRIDGE, BRISTOL.

4. The Old Drawbridge, c.1885. The ships are tied up at the quay, where the Centre gardens are now. In the middle distance can be seen John Wrights, printers. *(see illus. 166).* Husbands, the opticians, still trade on the corner of Denmark Street. Card by Burgess & Co., postally used in August 1909.

5. Old Bristol Harbour, 1871. A Fred Little picture, taken with the view towards the drawbridge. The small ship second from the right is a steamship amidst the sails. A delightful figurehead can be seen on the ship in the foreground.

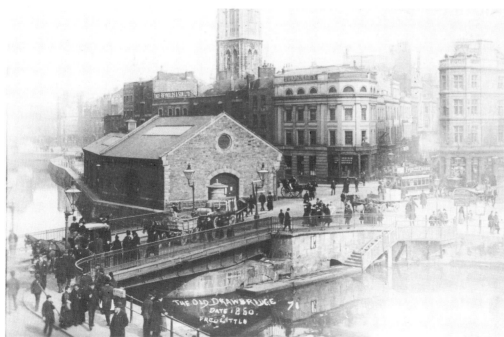

6. The Old Drawbridge, c.1880. This was replaced by a fixed bridge in 1892/3, when the river Froom, to the left of the picture, was covered over to form Magpie Park. The large shed, centre picture, was built in 1879, and the circular building in front of the shed was a watch box for the police. Thornley's hat shop, on the corner of Clare Street, was demolished in 1902, although the Thomas Reynold building remained until the 1950's. A lively, active scene, hansom cabs plying their trade, with a horse tram stopped near Baldwin Street. The notice to the right of the bridge advertises steam ferry boat trips, for 1/-. Another Fred Little production.

7. St. Augtustine's Place, c.1880. The picture was taken across the open water of the River Froom. The pawnbrokers' shop on the left of the picture became the Tramway Company offices. The Georgian building in the centre was formerly the Salem Chapel, the sign outside reading *"Davis, wood and ivory turner. All kinds of ship turning done"*. This building later became the home of the Salvation Army. It was demolished and replaced by offices for the Bristol Gas Co. The houses close by were replaced by a multi-storey car park in 1967. Park Row is at the top of the picture.

8. Broad Quay and Tramway Centre. This picture could have been taken from the crane used in the erection of the Co-op building, recently replaced by a newer building *(see illus. 1, volume 2)*. The tower of St. Stephen's can be seen piercing the skyline; buildings in the foreground have been replaced by the new Bristol and West building, and of course the Dublin shed has long gone. The postcard was sent from Bristol in November 1905.

BROAD QUAY and TRAMWAY CENTRE, BRISTOL.

9. Tramway Centre, c.1900. A very tranquil scene, of people strolling in the sunshine, very different from today's volume of traffic. The buildings on the left of the picture have changed very little, and Dunscombes and Husbands are still trading. A Midland Railway cart can be seen just behind the tram, wending its way into Anchor Road. Tram no. 178 is heading toward Hotwells, while the cart in the centre of the picture is being given a wide berth; evidently its contents are very unpleasant! Real photographic card by unidentified publisher.

10. The Centre and City Docks, September 1948. The time is 12.48 p.m. by the Tramway clock, and 12.45 p.m. by the C.W.S. clock! The river Froom was completely covered from the old St. Augustines Bridge to the Drawbridge, and became a car park. Now of course, we have the beautiful gardens. Postcard published in the R.A. series by un-named London firm.

11. The Centre, September 1948. The opposite view to illus. 10. The Sun Life building is on the corner of Clare Street, with Walker & Hall, silversmiths, taking one complete floor of the building. The stationary bus at the left of the picture is a utility Bedford HHU309. Can this be the same bus as seen right in the background of the previous picture? Card in the same series.

12. City Centre Gardens, early 1950's. The C.W.S. building has been replaced by a new imposing brick building, and the Unicorn hotel has been built overlooking the waterfront. Neptune can be seen on the Bridgehead. Postcard sent from Weymouth in July 1953.

13. Christmas Steps, formerly Queen Street, originally a steep and dangerous pathway outside the old city wall, until it was "steppered" in September 1669. Its quaintness remains, with some very attractive shops, selling antiques, prints, etc. Some lovely old gas lamps can be seen. Published by Viner.

Flower Market, Bristol.

14. Flower Market, c.1908. Built in 1745, it still retains its charm, and a gentle stroll through the market is rewarded with the delightful perfume of the flowers. All the buildings which can be seen through the archway were lost during the air raids of November 1940. A companion picture to illus. 18, volume 1.

15. Old Market Street, April, 1926. An excellent Garratt photograph showing the newly-built Central Hall. The barrow boys can be seen selling their wares outside the King's cinema, which has been demolished and an imposing office block erected in its place. According to the message on the back of the card, the "Scotch and Polly Company" were at the Empire Theatre just along the road. The tram is travelling to St. George from Bushy Park, Totterdown.

16. A view from the corner of Wine Street, looking toward Corn Street. All Saints church, the entrance of which is tucked away in All Saints Lane, leading to the flower market, is of Norman and 15th century architecture. It was rebuilt to its present state in 1711, designed by William Paul, who was greatly influenced by Wren. Next door to the church is a coffee house which has been in existence since 1713. The Norwich Union Life Insurance Society also used these premises for many years. Card published by Haywards of 1, Corn Street, Bristol.

"Hayward Series."   CORN STREET, BRISTOL.

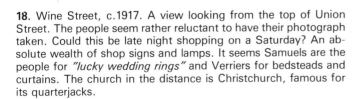

17. Wine Street, looking from Corn Street towards Union Street, with High Street to the right and Broad Street to the left. The Dutch House, and all the shops on the right of the picture, were destroyed during the air raids of November 1940. Jones & Co., an old and well-known firm of traders in Bristol are now titled Debenhams and trade in the Horsefair. The corner shop on the left is a tobacconist and the businesses away in the distance have been replaced by modern offices. A bustling scene, where the mode of transport seems to be either cart or bicycle!

18. Wine Street, c.1917. A view looking from the top of Union Street. The people seem rather reluctant to have their photograph taken. Could this be late night shopping on a Saturday? An absolute wealth of shop signs and lamps. It seems Samuels are the people for *"lucky wedding rings"* and Verriers for bedsteads and curtains. The church in the distance is Christchurch, famous for its quarterjacks.

19. Castle Street, c.1927. This view is taken looking up Castle Street toward Old Market Street, from Peters Street, (see volume 1 illus. 7). A card by the photographer Garratt which shows so clearly the appeal of "town". People could stroll and chat in safety, there were very few cars, and bicycles were ridden with care.

20. Castle Street, c.1928. This picture, by Hepworth, apparently taken from a top floor window, gives a superb view of this busy street. Garlicks, the outfitters, occupy a prominent corner, and the Regent Cinema, opened in July 1928, is sandwiched between Garlicks and Vernon Heaton Co, who are holding a £1 sale!

21. Castle Street in December 1936. Ten minutes past twelve on a busy afternoon! Cars were more numerous, crowds became heavier, so that on Saturdays all traffic was banned from the street. A lovely old Austin 7, registration no. HU 6495, slowly wends its way through the street. A child in a. pushchair looks longingly at the toys in the Home Stores window. The old Castle public house, with its shiny tile frontage, is next door. Perhaps the three men conversing in the foreground are debating whether to go in and have a quick one, while their wives do the shopping!

22. Victoria Street, c.1918. View taken looking towards Bristol Bridge. St. Nicholas church, with its rare Curfew clock, can be seen in the centre of the picture. A wonderful assembly of delivery carts, large and small, with Fry's cocoa very much in evidence. How about Mr. Wasley for teeth! Published by Viner of Bath.

START OF THE MAFEKING REJOICINGS.

23. Victoria Street, c.1900. Viewed in the opposite direction, towards Temple Meads. An early card, no.4 of a series presented by a magazine entitled *"Idle Moments"*, priced 1d. The celebrations were for a successful campaign during the Boer War.

24. Victoria Street, on a card published by Viner & Co. in 1919. This view was taken at the bottom of the incline of Temple Meads station, and it looks like summer time by the number of men wearing straw boaters! Brunel's old station, with its castle-like front, is to the right of the picture, with two Midland Railway carts on their way from the goods yard. The George and Grosvenor Hotels can be seen in the centre, with tram no.226 en route for Brislington.

25. Colston Street, Perry Road junction, c.1914. The trams were controlled by semaphore signals from the box built on the wall, and the signalman can be seen inside. Tram no.7 has just negotiated the hairpin bend from Colston Street into Perry Road. Tram no.163 approaches the bend en route for Westbury, and no.39 is climbing Upper Maudlin Street from the Horsefair and Old Market. The lines leading off centre foreground are from the underground stables.

26. St. Michael's Hill, on a postcard published in the 'Chatterton series' about 1921. The Children's Hospital, which was built in 1866, can just be seen on the left of the picture. The Headquarters of the 6th Battalion Gloster Regiment, opposite, is now the site of the new Bristol Maternity Hospital. The carter can be seen giving his horse a little help over the brow of the hill.

27. St. Michael's Hill, c.1908. A Fred Little picture of one of Bristol's most attractive streets, with a wonderful view of the city, although the skyline has altered somewhat over the years. Colston Almshouses, on the left, were founded in 1691 for the benefit of pensioners who were members of the Church of England, and had lived in Bristol for twenty years or more.

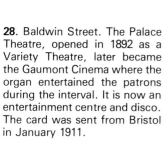

28. Baldwin Street. The Palace Theatre, opened in 1892 as a Variety Theatre, later became the Gaumont Cinema where the organ entertained the patrons during the interval. It is now an entertainment centre and disco. The card was sent from Bristol in January 1911.

THE PALACE THEATRE, BALDWIN STREET, BRISTOL.

29. High Street, c.1929. The signpost is situated on the cross of High Street, Bridge Street, Baldwin Street and Bristol Bridge. The top of the spire of Mary le Port church can just be seen above the Scholastic Trading Co. As can be seen by the size of the building, this was a very important firm of stationers and office suppliers. All these buildings were destroyed in 1940, just the tower of the church remaining. The ring on the top of the signpost states:-*"Bristol City and County"*. Message on reverse of card reads:- *"This is where your "Toys" came from!"*

30. Baldwin Street in Edwardian times. James Bigwood owned the fish and poultry premises, where wholesale and retail business was transacted. There was always a wonderful display of fish, with birds hanging from the rails. The firm was taken over by Saunders, and later Macfisheries, and closed in the early 1960's. This part of Baldwin Street was very busy as the wholesale fruit and vegetable trade was carried out here. It has now been transferred to the new market at St. Philips Marsh, though the fish trade is still carried out in St. Nicholas Street. No doubt used by the firm as a give-away advert card. This example was posted at Bath in November 1908.

JAMES BIGWOOD FISH GAME AND POULTRY SALESMAN, BALDWIN STREET, BRISTOL

31. St. James Churchyard. St. James Priory church on the left of the picture was built in 1130, with the tower being added in 1374. The spire of the Welsh church was removed in the 1950's, and an office block has been built between the two churches. Everyone on the top deck of the tram is wearing hats, as Edwardian fashion dictated.

32. The Old Horsefair, 1880, on a Fred Little photograph. As its name suggests, fairs were first held here in the Middle Ages, but were abolished in 1837. However, the vestry of St. James church reinstated the fair about 1900, with steam organs, side shows, galloping horses and all the fun of the fair! This is now the site of John Lewis's large store.

33. Lower Union Street, c.1920. Chamberlain Pole & Co. occupied the large corner building on the left. The buildings on the right hand side have been rebuilt: W.H. Smith occupy a large section in the middle, with Broadmead Chapel in the upper part. St. James Park is in the distance. This postcard is by the York Publishing Co.

34. North Street, Stokes Croft, published by Viner. This view is taken from the bottom of Stokes Croft looking toward the Horsefair. All the buildings have gone, and it is now a two-lane dual carriageway. The Full Moon Hotel, seen in the centre of the picture, is the only building left. This is the opposite view to illus. 31, volume 1.

35. Stokes Croft: the top of the Croft, looking towards Cheltenham Road. Wonderful array of meat hanging outside Edwards the butcher. The sign on the wall of the shop states *"families waited on daily, corned beef and pickled tongues supplied"*. The delivery boy poses for the cameraman before going on his way, and the little boy with a sailor hat on looks quite bewildered! Altogether eight horse-drawn vehicles are parked at the curb, and not a traffic warden in sight!

36. Jamaica Street, looking towards Stokes Croft, with Thomas Street on the left. A good crowd is waiting for the parade of the Naval Reservists. The building centre right was part of the Baptist College, now gone, although the shop in the centre of the picture remains. The postcard is of 1915 vintage.

37. Lower Ashley Road, looking towards what is now the roundabout over the M32, from Sussex Place and Ashley Road. The Lord Nelson is now a builders' merchant, with a modern garage just beyond. The two little girls in smocks pose for the camera, and are the boys playing marbles? Photographic postcard by unidentified publisher.

38. Ashley Road, Salvation Army Headquarters, on a card postally used from Coventry in 1911. The headquarters were opened in 1896, the original building having been destroyed by fire in 1893. Part of the building has been demolished, and a modern extension erected; only the far building with the pointed roof remains.

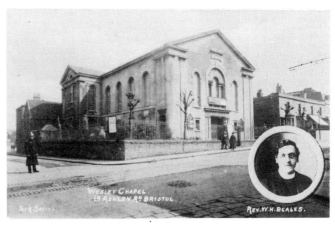

39. Lower Ashley Road: the Wesleyan Chapel on the crossroads of Pennywell Road and Mina Road, an area that went completely when the roundabout over the M32 was built in the early 1970's. The chapel was built in 1837, and can be seen in the middle distance of illus. 37. Postcard in the 'York' series.

40. Grosvenor Road, about 1920. All the buildings on the left of the picture were cleared in the early 1970's, and so were the shops on the right hand side, with the exception of the corner shop, which is at the junction of Grosvenor Road and St. Nicholas Road. Card published in the 'Chatterton series' by A. G. Short & Co.

41. Ashley Road, with the junction of Grosvenor Road. Looking the opposite way in Grosvenor Road to illus. 40. The corner property in the centre of the picture has been demolished. Note the advertisement for Rogers' Special Stout, 2/6d (12½p) per dozen bottles or 1/6d (7½p) for a dozen half bottles! Published by Viner of Bath.

42. Ashley Road, on a card posted in Bristol 2nd October, 1920. Taken further back from illus. 41 above, with the Metropole cinema, which opened in 1913, and closed in 1968, on the right. Note the model T Ford passing the horse and cart. Another A.G. Short postcard.

43. Hotwells. St. Peter's church and parish hall on a view looking towards the present roundabout in Hotwell Road. Jacobs Wells Road is off to the right. All the buildings have been demolished and replaced by modern flats. The trees are now mature and still a feature there.

44. Mardyke Ferry, Hotwells. The ferry was used to cross from Hotwell Road to Cumberland Road and vice-versa, and although this has long since been discontinued, a motor boat ferry service is in operation at points around the floating harbour. Several Campbells pleasure steamers can be seen moored along both quays.

45. Dowry Parade, once a very select area. The lovely Georgian houses still grace the Parade today. Away in the distance is Dowry Square, whose large houses were once owned by some of the wealthy merchants of Bristol: an elegant Square with trees in the centre gardens. Humphrey Davey, who invented the miners lamp lived here. The Parade is now part of the one-way traffic system from the Cumberland Basin flyover. Published by Viner.

CITY DOCKS

46. Hotwell Docks. This view is taken from near or on the roof of one of the tobacco bond warehouses adjoining the Cumberland Basin. The row of cottages to the left of the tall chimney is still lived in and with their bright tubs of flowers outside form a very attractive sight. The name of this waterside pathway is Nova Scotia. A large timber yard can be seen to the right of the picture; this was owned by Taylor Low Bros at Canada Wharf. Part of the area still houses timber, and a very pleasant caravan area has been laid out further on, along with small blocks of flats, very much in keeping with the area. Postcard by Harvey Barton & Son Ltd.

47. Bristol Harbour, looking toward Prince Street swing bridge. The old Bush tea warehouse can be seen centre right; this is now used by the Arnofini for arts of all kinds. On the skyline can be seen the towers of Bristol Cathedral and Cabot Tower. Postcard used in 1913.

48. Bristol Docks. Another interesting view of the City docks taken from where the Industrial Museum has been set up. The Bush warehouse is very prominent and there are many types of shipping berthed at the quay.

S.S. GREAT BRITAIN

THE HISTORICAL OLD "GREAT BRITAIN" COMPLETING 85 YEARS CONTINUOUS SERVICE FINALLY AT REST. PORT STANLEY, FALKLAND ISLANDS.

49. S.S. Great Britain. The first iron steamship ever, designed by I.K. Brunel, and launched from Bristol in 1843. For 30 years she was a passenger ship, and in later years a cargo ship. In 1886, damaged by storms while on a voyage from Penarth to San Francisco, she put into Port Stanley in the Falkland Islands. She was never to go to sea again and was finally beached at Sparrow Cove. There was great interest for her return to Bristol, a fund was launched and with Jack Hayward giving generously, the huge operation to bring her "home" was under way, and culminated in her return in 1970. Her restoration had begun! This photographic card sports a Falkland Islands stamp on the picture side.

50. This picture shows how badly the Great Britain had deteriorated. She is being restored in her original dry dock.

51. This view of the hull shows the very fine line of the ship. Much has been accomplished and she is looking "great" again.

52. Cheltenham Road. A Viner card of Arley Chapel, at the junction of Arley Hill on the left and Bath buildings on the right. The corner shops on the right were removed for road widening, and a garage and forecourt occupy the site today. The chapel is used as a place of worship by the Polish community in Bristol.

53. Free Library, Cheltenham Road. This was opened on 24th March, 1877, was burnt down during World War II, and rebuilt as a single storey building. It is the present north district library. The railway arch carries the Temple Meads to Severn Beach line. The postcard was sent from Bristol in June 1909.

54. Zetland and Gloucester Road junction. In the past, this area has been very susceptible to flooding from the Cran Brook. The floods captured in this picture occurred in July 1914. The tram depot is now a modern shop, formerly Morgans, Colmers and today Home Plan, a furniture store. The cart belonged to a firm which supplied shops with ginger beer, hop ale, sasparilla and burdock, all in stone bottles.

GLOUCESTER ROAD

55. Gloucester Road, looking north, with Elton Road on the left. It's still a very busy shopping thoroughfare. The shops have been modernised while retaining the old upper sections of the buildings. A modern wine store stands where the trees are in the picture. Card by Viner.

56. Gloucester Road. Bristol North Baths are on the right of the picture, next door the Horfield Inn, now called the 'Bristol Flyer'. The houses have disappeared and shops have been built there. Plenty of room for the cyclists! Postcard published by W.H. Smith in their 'Grosvenor' series.

57. Gloucester Road. A more leisurely view than today. Pearce's hardware shop is still trading today, and the Old Fox is centre right. The large building in the distant centre is Lloyds Bank, on the corner of Dongola Road. Very difficult to find a parking place along here (or any other part of Gloucester Road) today. This card dates from about 1910.

58. Gloucester Road, c.1910, at the junction with Filton Avenue and Wellington Hill. The boys playing in the road (what children could play there now?) appear to be wearing the uniform of Mullers orphanage, and some of them realise their photograph is being taken. The buildings here are unchanged.

59. Gloucester Road tram depot, c.1910. This depot was opened in 1892, twelve years after the experiment of using steam trams to conquer the gradients of Gloucester Road. Decorated, perhaps for a Royal visit?

60. The interior of the Horfield tram depot. A lovely photograph of the workers. Incredible how very much alike they all are, with their mufflers, caps and moustaches!

Redland Hill, Bristol.

61. A view looking up Redland Hill, with the trees of Redland Green in the centre. The tram, no.40, with its conductress (which dates this picture 1917-1919), is travelling to Durdham Down. The houses and gardens are much the same, with the more modern business premises of A.C. Stone & Co. Postcard by A.G. Short & Co.

62. Coldharbour Road. The open fields in the distance mark the beginning of Kellaway Avenue, which was opened in 1921, the houses being built in the late 1920's and early 1930's, including Springfield Grove. Traffic lights have replaced the white sign post. 'York series' postcard.

Coldharbour Road, Redland, 330.

63. Zetland Road: this view, looking towards Zetland Road junction, from the corner of Redland Road has not changed very much over the years. In the middle distance is the suburb of St. Andrews, one of the prosperous districts of Bristol. The houses were built around the park, which was opened in 1895. (See illus. 180 vol. 1). Postcard by Hardings, postally used in September 1904.

Zetland Road, Redland, Bristol.   No. 533.   5. 9. 1904.

CLIFTON

64. Blackboy Hill. This view, taken from the corner of Apsley Road, shows an elegant, bustling shopping area, with tram no.21 on its way to Eastville. Although this is a continuation of Whiteladies Road, it is always known as Blackboy Hill, after the inn of that name, which was removed in the 1890's for road widening, (see illus. 67 vol.1). Card posted from Bristol in January 1906.

65. Whiteladies Road: on the left of the picture can be seen the former Imperial Hotel, now called Canynge House, and used by Bristol University. The entrance to Clifton Down Station runs along the side of the hotel. The tower rising above the shops belongs to Tyndale Baptist church. The shops on the left have been demolished, and a new shopping centre erected. W.H. Smith postcard, used in October 1912.

66. Clifton Down Station. On the 15th May 1907, the Colonial Premiers visited Bristol to view the progress of the building of the Royal Edward dock at Avonmouth. This photograph shows the arrival of the procession at the station incline. According to the local report in the newspaper, the *"route was lined throughout with thousands of people, the weather being very fine"*. Those in the procession included:- Premier of Canada - Sir Wilfred Laurier & Lady Laurier; Premier of New Zealand - St. Joseph Ward; Premier of Newfoundland - Sir. Robert Bond; Premier of Natal -The Right Honourable F.R. Moor, and representatives of Australia and elsewhere.

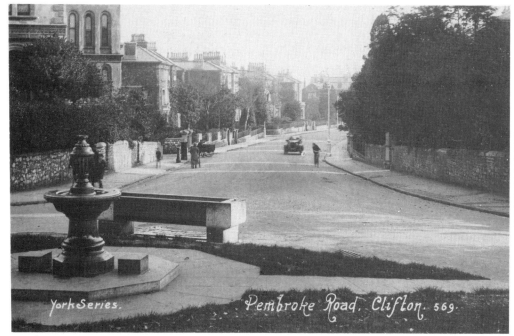

67. Pembroke Road, Clifton, a lovely road that has changed little over the years; the large houses are mostly converted into flats and it is a very busy thoroughfare to the Downs and beyond. 'York series' postcard of c.1920.

68. West Mall, Clifton. The postcard was published by Viner of Bath, and sold by S.J. Thomas of Boyces Avenue, Clifton. Situated just off the Mall, a very elegant row of Georgian town houses. Time has stood still here, except for the fact that boys cannot stand around in the road posing for a photographer because of the traffic. The young butcher boy has moved away from his delivery bicycle to strike a better pose. A lovely Daimler can just be seen on the left, reg. AE1490.

69. Clifton Park, on a card posted in January 1913, a very attractive road running through to Pembroke Road. The photograph was taken from Canynge Road. Apart from the trees in the gardens having been thinned out, and the creepers removed from the walls of the houses, it is quite unchanged.

70. Henleaze Road. This card, posted in August 1920, was written by a lady who lived about halfway along the road. Her message reads: *"We arrived home quite safely, had to stand all the way from Exeter! X marks the spot".* The trees and gardens on the left have been removed for road widening. Shops include Watkins the Drapers, and Henry Baker, confectioners.

71. This picture was taken on the corner of Henleaze Road. The gentlemen portrayed are Mr. Tedder, standing outside his office, with Mr. Hendy, the relieving officer. Lake Road, situated by the signpost, was a roadway leading to a quarry, which is now owned by Henleaze Swimming Club.

72. Henleaze Road. This view, looking in the same direction as illus. 71, would have been taken about 1921, before road widening had taken place. The cottages on the right have been removed, but the rank of cottages on the left survive today.

Rockleaze Road, Sneyd Park.

Sincock, The Library, Sneyd Park.

73. Rockleaze Road, Sneyd Park. A view not greatly changed: this is still a busy row of shops today. When this card was posted at Clifton in 1906, though, the style of dress was certainly different, and bicycles, rather than parked cars, predominate. The rear of the large Rockleaze houses are showing in the background on this card, and the mews to the left have been converted into homes. The postcard was published by Thomas and Sincock, who owned Rockleaze Post Office, featured in the picture.

74. Stoke Bishop village centre with the Tagart fountain, built to celebrate Queen Victoria's Jubilee. A road was built in 1925 to take traffic away from the old narrow road in the foreground - this latter became a cul-de-sac in 1970. The house in the background was the house of John Chetwood-Aitken, but was demolished in 1934 for the Druid Hill shops. The signpost points the way to Sea Mills Railway Station (left) and Shirehampton and Avonmouth (right). 'Chatterton' series postcard by A.G. Short & Co.

STOKE VILLIAGE, NR. BRISTOL.

Sneyd Park from Sea Walls.

75. A view of the Sea Mills area of Sneyd Park, taken from the Downs. The mansion on the right (Towerhurst) survives today, but Sea Walls Villa, next to it, was demolished for Sea Walls flats in the 1970's, though the lodges remain. Several of the large mansions became schools, were used for other institutional purposes, taken down to be replaced by modern blocks of luxury flats, or converted to flats or nursing homes.

Wells Rd. Knowle.

No.1

76. Wells Road, Knowle, c.1910, on a Harvey Barton postcard. Tram no.72 is travelling toward the George Hotel at the top of the hill. Belluton Road is off to the left, with the cyclist just passing the end of it. Young trees in the picture have now grown to maturity, and houses have been built on the space behind the trees.

Wells Road Knowle Bristol   AGS&Co 312

77. Wells Road. Superb photographic card in the "Chatterton" series, published by A.G. Short & Co. Tram no. 208, service 10 is travelling from Knowle to Bristol Bridge, with a conductress and an inspector. The cottage next to the inn later became a newsagents, but was blitzed during world war 2. The gentlemen in the lovely cart could be off-duty milkmen. Card postally used in August 1918.

78. Wells Road on a Harvey Barton card, looking south towards Broad Walk and Red Lion Hill. The large house on the left is now Cleeve House school, and in the distance can be seen the rooftop of the Weslyan Chapel (on the corner of Redcatch Road), and St. Martins church.

79. This part of Wells Road is still recognisable today. The Post Office is housed in the second shop on the right, and the structure is virtually the same. The new shopping centre and small shops have taken over from the first tram wire poles. The weather hasn't changed either: message reads *"Very cold at Weston today, and a snowstorm in the morning"*. The month was April! 'York series' postcard, sent from Bristol in 1924.

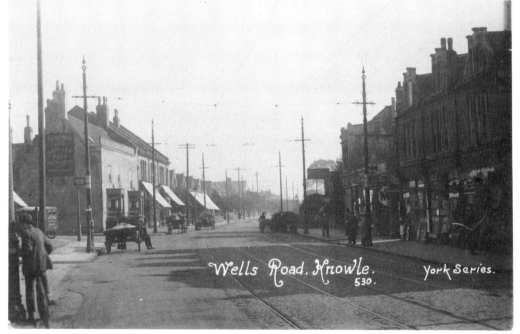

80. Knowle Cricket Ground. 'Bee' series postcard published by Burgess & Co., and posted in 1923.

81. The Pavilion, Knowle Cricket ground. The cricket ground is situated at the top of Broad Walk, and some very exciting matches are still played here. The old pavilion has recently been replaced by a splendid brick construction. This area was once the site of the Knowle race-course, which was opened in 1873. The grandstand, which accommodated 3,000 people, was roughly where Redcatch Park now is. Kind Edward VII, when Prince of Wales, attended the opening meeting. This postcard was published by Harvey Barton.

BRISLINGTON

82. Grove Road and Belle Vue, Brislington. This view, taken from St. Lukes church tower, shows Grove Road along the bottom of the picture; this has been re-named Hollywood Road. The large building centre foreground is the Pilgrim Inn, and the lane in front of it is Freeland alley. The roof and bell tower of the United Reform church can be seen at the top left of the picture.

83. Montrose Avenue, Brislington. This road runs from Wick Road to Fry's Alley, at the side of the Pilgrim Inn (see illus. 82). The tower of St. Lukes church can be seen. The large house in the middle distance was, in 1799, a boarding school for "sons of Gentlemen", and became St. Lukes vicarage in 1896. It has now been converted into flats. The card was sent in March 1914.

84. Delightfully tranquil scene in what was once known as Grove Road, (see illus. 82). The 'Kings Arms' Inn stands on the left corner, with the smithy on the right. Adverts on the wall of the smithy tell of firms which have long since disappeared. A small child in a wicker push-chair is being taken for a walk, while the horse waits patiently.

85. Wick House, Brislington. Three cards of a series issued pre-1914. Wick House as seen in this picture was built in the 1790's, set in approximately 60 acres of ground. One prominent occupier, in 1881, was Thomas Harding of Colthurst & Harding, paint manufacturers. Most of the land was built on after World War I, and in 1924, it became the property of the Church of England Childrens Society, and it continued to be a children's home until a few years ago, when it became a nursing home for elderly people.

86. Aviary, Wick House. This was situated in the grounds behind the house.

87. The Lodge, Wick House. This could be seen from Sandy Park Road. The large gate behind the little girl was the entrance to the drive to the house. The lodge was demolished in 1931 for the building of houses in Allison Road.

88. Arno's Castle. First of three cards of a series issued by Little & Barber, buyers of old English furniture, and works of art. The Bath house was built in 1765, and could be reached from Arno's Court by a tunnel under the road. The frontage was removed in 1957 and re-erected at Portmerion, North Wales.

89 & 90. The interior of the Bath House, before and after the alterations had been made. It was demolished in 1965, and a snooker hall is now established on the site.

91. Water Lane, Brislington. Runs from the top of Bristol Hill through to West Town Lane. Once a peaceful country lane, where a boy could sail his paper boat, with baby sister watching from the push chair. This lane is now filled with houses, and the new Tesco superstore occupies the old Robertsons jam factory site. Postcard by J. Thompson of Belfast.

92. Comer's shop on the corner of Winchester Road and Sandy Park Road. Mr. Comer's brother owned the ironmongers and post office at the other end of Winchester Road. The picture shows some well-stocked windows, with *"fine new currants 3d per lb. Splendid sultanas 4d per lb."* Photographic card by un-named publisher, posted from Bristol in December 1905.

93. Talbot Lane, Brislington. Harvey Barton card, postally used in August 1916. This is now called Talbot Road, leading from Knowle to Brislington Village, although it is still known as the 'Lane' by many people born in Brislington.

94. The Rock, which can be reached from Sherwell Road. The cottage in the foreground has been demolished, but the one at the rear has been extended and modernised. Oil lamps were in existence until electricity was installed. The card was posted in July 1916.

95. St. Anne's church, Brislington. The postcard shows the church before the chancel and sanctuary were built, and to the right, between the church and houses in Langton Road, the "iron mission church", which was built in 1903, can be seen. This mission church was dismantled and re-erected at the top of Sandy Park, near what is now Allison Road.

96 and 97. The exterior and interior of St. Anne's Church, when it was a temporary church for St. Cuthberts, until a permanent church was erected in 1933. Part of this temporary building was then taken to the Pear Tree in Ironmould Lane for use as a cricket pavilion by St. Cuthberts cricket club.

98. Redcliffe Street, c.1930, by the photographer Garratt. This view is looking toward St. Mary Redcliffe church, with Jay's furnishing store on the left, next door to the Temperance Hotel. The shaft of sunlight across the road comes from Freshford Lane. Some buildings on the left remain, but those on the right are all demolished.

99. Bedminster Bridge, c.1900. Once called Harford Bridge, this card shows a far more peaceful scene than today's hustle and bustle. The message on the back of the card says it all:- *"Dear Evie, how much money did you win? I'll have a small beer and some chitling if you want to treat me. I expect your mother will know this place, it is showing Redcliffe church and next door to the Public (George and Dragon), is Redcliffe Almshouses. Do you think you would like to live there?"* All the shops and houses have given way to flats and offices.

100. Redcliffe Hill, on a postcard used on 24th August 1909. Taken further up the hill from illus. 99, showing the variety of shops. E.W. Hill, the chemist on the left of the picture advertises *"Coles neuralgic cure, gives instant relief"*. Also visible are Harris, pastrycook and confectioner, and a hair cutting room. On the right people's eating habits seem to be well-catered for: refreshment rooms, a small inn and People's Dining rooms, where again, cyclists were welcome. One very famous place here was the faggot and pea shop, with the large square copper pan bubbling away in the window. Photographic card by anonymous publisher.

101. Redcliffe Hill. Continuing from illus. 100, the pavement rises before graduating towards the Shot Tower where lead shot was first invented. The building was demolished in 1968, having originally been built in the late 1780's. A new Shot Tower was built in Cheese Lane in 1968.

102. View from St. Mary Redcliffe churchyard. The glass cone, which dominates the picture, was built in 1780. It was originally 120 feet high, but the upper part was removed in 1936 because it was proved to be unsafe. The ground floor is now used as a restaurant, the Kiln.

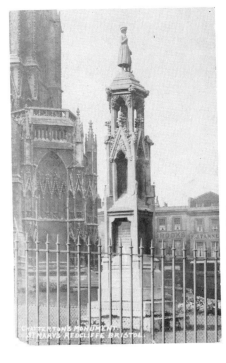

103. Chattertons monument, a statue dedicated to Thomas Chatterton, the boy poet, who lived in Pylle Street, (now Redcliffe Way), in 1752. He committed suicide at the tender age of 18. The statue was erected in 1840. Designed by F.C. Fripp, it cost £100, and was 31 feet in height, but by 1967 it was beyond repair, and was destroyed. A Mr. Chandler, who was apprenticed to a firm of builders working on St. Mary Redcliffe, was dressed as a Colston School boy and used as a model for the statue. A plaque to the memory of Chatterton can be found in the south transept of his beloved church. Postcard sent from Bristol in August 1914.

BEDMINSTER

104. Bedminster Bridge, in the 'Chatterton series', published by A.G. Short and Co., on a card postally used in 1912. This view is taken from York Road, showing the General Hospital and the Granary at Princes Wharf in the distance. Pines the grocers were on the corner of York Road and Bedminster Parade.

105. North Street, looking toward Cannon Street, with a tram travelling to Ashton Gate. This is still a very busy shopping area, and is virtually unchanged. Willways Dye Works are very much in evidence, also the Singer Sewing Machine company. No publisher indicated.

106. West Street, looking toward St. John's Road and Robinson building, now the home of Don Cameron's balloons. The Theatre Royal playbill advertises Mr. Ernest Carpenter's *"Shadows of a great city"*, beginning Monday 19th July, 1909. Ironmonger Mr. G. Steinberg, advertises *"old couches made as new, 8/6d"*. Next door, Mr. Smith makes rick covers, loin cloths and tarpaulins etc; and for your soul, the Christian Mission provides the answer! Another superb photographic card.

107. Tramway Junction, East Street, Bedminster. Published by Viner & Co., c.1914. A lively scene at the junction of East Street and Cannon Street. This corner is commonly known as the London Inn, taking its name from the public house on the corner, where this picture was taken. In the foreground can be seen a small milk delivery cart, with the churn balancing in the centre. Boots the chemist now have a shop further down on the left hand side of East Street. Many interesting trade signs, even one urging people *"not to take drugs, use a natural remedy, Herbs"*.

108. Bedminster Hippodrome, in the 'Chatterton series', published by A.G.S. & Co. This is a continuation of East Street, roughly in the middle, and always a hive of activity. Sadly, the Hippodrome is no longer a part of its life. It opened in 1911 as a Music Hall; the proprietor was Walter de Frese. When later it became a cinema, the name was changed to the Stoll Picture House. The large cart on the left appears to be a cattle transporter.

109. East Street, Bedminster. We have now come to the end of this very busy thoroughfare. The police station, with its castle-like appearance, can be seen along the right of the picture. A cabbies' rest is near the trees, above which can be seen the roof of Zion Chapel, founded by one John Hare. At the present time this is being converted into offices, keeping the original facade.

SOUTHVILLE

110. Beauley Road, Southville. Real photograph, published by Viner and postally used in July 1918. Unchanged over the years, although much busier now. The church on the left is St. David's, whose foundation stone was laid by Lady Smyth on 2nd November, 1908. Raleigh Road goes off to the right. The registration number of the motor bike and sidecar in the front of the picture is AE 660.

111. Coronation Road, Southville. A Hepworth photo, postally used in March 1934. This road was so named after George IV opened it in 1822: a road of elegant houses, many of them now converted into flats. St. Pauls church, which suffered during the blitz, was rebuilt in 1950.

112. Vauxhall Footbridge, viewed from Cumberland Road, looking across the river to Coronation Road. A tug is steaming up the New Cut. This pedestrian swing bridge has now been permanently fixed. Postcard by W.F. Brisley, and sent from Bristol in October 1910.

113. London Midland Railway. A view of the engine sheds at Barrow Road, on a photograph taken 23rd July, 1939. All the houses have gone, as also the wonderful, dirty days of steam.

114. Lawrence Hill, c.1900. Children are posing for the photographer on the bridge over the Midland line of the railway, and a bread delivery cart has stopped just before the Pack Horse Hotel. Next door is Colston's the undertaker. Lovely advert for Snowball flour, Veribest! An extremely scarce postcard.

115. Lawrence Hill, coming up from Clarence Road to Lawrence Hill station. The spire in the background belongs to St. Lawrence church. Butter is advertised at 1/6d per lb, and the Waverley Vaults, proprietor W. Jay, can be seen on the left of the picture. The card was sent from Bristol in August 1912.

AVONMOUTH

116. Avonmouth. The park was the gift of Mr. Napier Miles. It's a small park, but a delightful open space in the heart of industrial dockland. The church is St. Andrews, and the bandstand has long since gone. Postcard by T. Harding.

117. Avonmouth Road, on a card posted in August 1921 and published by Viner. This view shows the park on the right, looking towards the docks, which were opened in 1877. The delivery cart is owned by the Bristol Co-operative Society.

118. Gloucester Road, Avonmouth, looking towards the level crossing of the Temple Meads to Severn Beach line, near Avonmouth station. Spillers' flour mill can be seen in the background. The milk delivery cart on the left sold milk from large churns, measured into customers' own jugs. The postcard was sent to the Chief Officer, M.V. British Hope, The Docks, Falmouth, posted from Avonmouth in May 1935.

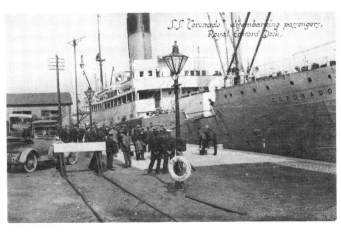

119. The "Royal Edward" at Avonmouth. The arrival of this boat at the very busy passenger terminal was quite an event. This picture is dated April 1910, just two years after King Edward VII officially opened the Royal Edward Dock. Card by Harvey Barton & Son Ltd.

120. The S.S. "Coronado". One of a series of cards published by the Port of Bristol to commemorate the British Empire Exhibition in 1924.

121. The Royal Edward Dock. An excellent aerial view of a corner of this dock. The cargo discharged by these ships would consist of timber, tobacco, bananas, etc. Valentine of Dundee published the card.

122. Granaries at Avonmouth. A card issued by the Port of Bristol Authority, showing the facilities available for the storage of grain, after the cargo has been discharged from the ships. A clear aerial view, looking across the Bristol Channel.

FISHPONDS

123. Briar Way. A new housing estate, built in the late 1920's and early 1930's, a period of immense building of council houses. This picture would date around 1932. A young boy taking his baby brother or sister out in the pram can be seen on the right. Postcard in the 'York' series.

124. Fishponds Road, showing Elmgrove Post Office. At the bottom of Lodge Causeway is tram no.140 on its way to Fishponds from the Tramway Centre.

125. Fishponds Road, looking towards Station Road centre left, with the forecourt of the Full Moon Hotel, an early taxi, and Hodders the chemist, behind the taxi cab stand. Delightful group of children on the right of the picture posing for the photographer, each with their own fashion in headgear! Posted from Fishponds in May 1913.

126. Southmead Road Post Office & supply stores (proprietor E. Banfield) established in 1885, at 316 Southmead Road. This card, published by Viner and posted in 1915, long before road widening, bears this message:- *"You will see me standing with a black kitten in my arms. . . . "* It is sent to a trained soldier at Caterham Depot.

127. The entrance to Southmead Hospital in Southmead Road, when it was known as the 2nd Southern Hospital. The buildings remain the same, although the entrance has been enlarged and the road widened. The soldiers in the middle of the road look to be going for a swim; they appear to have towels around their necks. Another Viner card.

128. A view of some of the wards of the formerly named 2nd Southern Hospital Southmead, showing some of the wounded soldiers of World War I, recovering from their injuries. These buildings, although modernised, are still in use today. Photo by Garratt, postally used in March 1917.

FRENCHAY

129. The village of Frenchay before it was included within the Bristol City boundary. The Post Office is now closed, but the street which leads down to the river Froom is unchanged. The lady in black appears very prim and proper, and the boy by her side looks none too happy either; perhaps his stiff collar is pinching! Card no. 336 in Hardings' 'Progress' series, posted at Clifton in March 1906.

FRENCHAY, NEAR BRISTOL.
The "Progress" Series, No. 336.

T. H. S & Co., B & C.

130. Tea Gardens, Frenchay. By the river Froom: a delightful view showing one of the many tea gardens. The cottage in the distance has a sign which reads:- *"Frenchay edge tool and file works"*, one of the village industries. A Garratt postcard, no.476.

TEA GARDENS 476.
FRENCHAY BRISTO

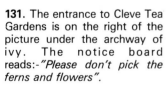

131. The entrance to Cleve Tea Gardens is on the right of the picture under the archway of ivy. The notice board reads:-*"Please don't pick the ferns and flowers"*.

CLEVE TEA GARDENS
FRENCHAY 336

132. Soundwell Road, a long winding road, virtually unchanged over the years, running from Two Mile Hill to the old City boundary.

133. Downend. These Cottage homes were the pioneers of small family homes for orphans. They are now closed, although their closure was delayed for a while after protests from the young people living there. Postcard published by J.C. Young of Redfield.

134. Downend. A quiet view of North Street, as it leaves the centre of Downend village, looking towards Cleeve Hill. 'York' series postcard, with 1920 postal usage.

135. St. George. A view taken about 1902-3. The iron church has been dismantled, and houses now cover the grassy area. Nags Head Hill, with the Air Balloon Tavern, can be seen in the centre distance.

136. An unusual advertising card of the Pied Horse Hotel, St. George, with a photograph of the landlord, Will Hanns, in the centre. The inn is situated at Summerhill Road, and is still flourishing.

137. St. George. The bay-fronted villas of Hudd's Hill Road are typical of the houses built at the turn of the century. The road connects with Whiteway Road and Ventnor Road.

138. Zion Chapel, on the corner of Grantham Road, was a chapel much associated with music in the Kingswood district. Samuel Burchill, for many years their music master, entered their choir at the first Bristol Music Festival, in 1873. He organised many concerts at the chapel in aid of the poor. It is now the Kingswood Methodist Church. W.H. Smith 'Grosvenor series' postcard.

139. This delightful card shows the tennis courts at the park in Kingswood. No short skirts or shorts for these tennis players! The older houses in the centre or the picture remain, but modern houses have been built either side of the road, and the tennis courts are no more. 'York' series card, posted in September 1922.

140. Kingswood High Street, looking directly down towards Warmley Hill, with the wall of Kingswood Parish Church on the right. The shops have survived and are still in business today. Another 'York' series publication.

141. Hanham Road, Kingswood, with Moravian Road off to the left. The houses to the right still stand, but the cottage on the corner has been replaced by industry, the premises of Lucas Technical Dept. The sign on the old cottage reads:- *"Breaks, Waggonettes, landaus, traps to let or hire. Break outings catered for"*. The card was posted in January 1907.

142. Cossham Memorial Hospital. This was built as a memorial to Hadel Cossham, who owned coal mines in Kingswood, two being Speedwell and Deep Pit. This hospital is a landmark, as it is built on one of the highest hills in Bristol. Posted in 1908 and sent to a private in the 2nd Coy. D.C.L.I. in Bermuda.

143. Superb photograph of Regent Street, Kingswood, looking towards the clock tower, and taken in the late afternoon, with a group of paper-boys waiting for the unloading of the *Evening World* van. This was a local paper which was first published in 1929. The *Evening Post* began publication in 1932, and there was intense competition between the two papers. The *Evening World* offered a bonus of 5/- for blue seals collected from 18 newspapers and many other gift schemes; it finally closed in 1962. The *Evening Post* is still going strong.

LONGWELL GREEN

Longwell Green Village.

144. Longwell Green Village. This is a view looking towards Willsbridge Hill and Bath. All Saints church can be seen on the left. The road has been widened and many modern houses built in and around the village. The postcard was published by E. Pomeray at Longwell Green Post Office, and posted in 1912.

145. Longwell Green. This barn at Court Farm, which is situated at the end of Court Farm Road, is named "Sally on the Barn", because of the statue on the top of the tower. To reach it, take the left turn at the top of Willsbridge Hill. A charming rural scene on a postcard with 1913 postal usage.

SALLY ON THE BARN, LONGWELL GREEN. 6.

THE MILL, CATSCLIFF, WILLSBRIDGE   A. A. Adams, P.O., Oldland Common

146. Willsbridge. This mill has been restored, and with the park and woodland around it, has been opened to the public as a museum and wild life information centre. With the river Boyd running alongside, it is a very pleasant place. When this picture was taken it was a working mill: note the interesting, triangular-shaped dove cote on the wall. Published by A.A. Adams, Post Office, Oldland Common, and posted in February 1905.

EARLY CARDS

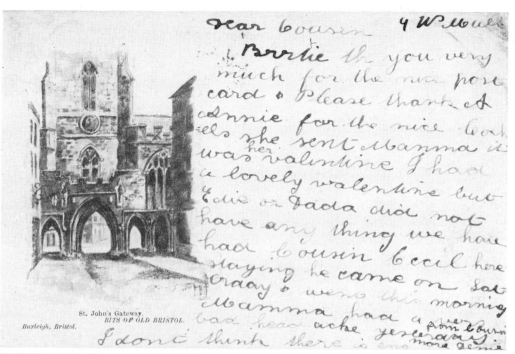

147. St. John's Gateway, printed by Burleigh in their series "Bits of Old Bristol", and posted in 1903.

148. Colston Avenue; card posted in Greenock 13/11/03, and with a second handstamp New Greenock 14/11/03.

149. St. Augustine's Bridge, court size, postally used 6/12/1900.

150. Lawrence Hill Station, opened in 1863, on the Bristol & South Wales Railway, via New Passage Ferry. This was replaced by the Severn Tunnel in 1886. Lawrence Hill is still in use for the Severn Beach Line and Gloucester line. J.C. Young postcard, sent in June 1907.

151. Bedminster Station, the first out of Temple Meads, opened in 1870 for passengers travelling to the West Country. Rebuilt in the 1930's, when extra lines were added. Still open for limited passenger service only, but the bridge and waiting rooms have all been removed; just the platforms remain. This C.S. & Co. postcard was actually posted at Paddington in August 1905, announcing the safe arrival of a traveller.

152. Joint Railway Station, Avonmouth. Superb Viner photograph, with rather a poignant message on the back:- *"I have to send this one for Sonny and tell you to come home, he is waiting for the Royal George to come in"*. This station was opened on 1st September, 1885, and major re-building took place in 1926. Goods trains ceased to use the line in June 1966.

PEOPLE

153. Madam Clara Butt, the famous singer, graced the Empire celebrations at Ashton Gate, in 1911. Top hats and ladies' flowered and be-ribboned hats are very much in evidence. The photographer was H.E. Smith, and the card published in the 'Chatterton' series by A.G. Short.

154. The Entertainer Sydney Bishop of Knowle. An unusual autographed photograph. Can any of our readers enlighten us regarding this gentleman? The card is dated 12.2.1918.

155. Rev. J. Trebilco. This gentleman, the Pastor of Russell Town Congregational Church, and the following men were the founders of St. George Higher Grade School (see illus. 128 vol.2):- Albert George Verrier, master tailor. James William Jones, a coach-builder of Kingswood. Joseph Bateman, grocer. Edmund Harvey, grocer, and George Cambridge, bootmaker. A lovely message on the front of the card :- *"This is the Parson that gave me your pretty sister to keep"*. Posted at Bath in September 1907.

ENTRANCE LODGE, ASHTON COURT.

156. Ashton Court. One of the entrance lodges to the Ashton Court estate. The lovely mansion and the estate were purchased by the City Council for everyone to enjoy. C.S. & Co. postcard, used in June 1909.

157. The Mansion House, Ashton Court. There has been a manor house here since Saxon times, being one of the four manors of Long Ashton. It was bought by John Smyth in 1545. The right side of the present building dates from 1615, while the left side dates from 1765. Card posted in December 1912.

Ashton Court. South Front.

158. Ashton Court. A photograph of Dame Emily Smyth at the west door of the mansion, c.1910. She was the wife of Sir Greville Smyth, Bt. who died in 1901.

AIRCRAFT

159. Filton. Bristol biplane, c.1910. The Bristol Boxkite was the first aircraft to be built by the Bristol & Colonial Airplane Co. In September 1910, an improved model, with a more powerful engine was built, with a top speed of 37 m.p.h.

160. The flight of M. Tetard over Clifton Suspension Bridge. A Bristol Boxkite, probably the fourteenth to be built, was completed at Filton on 9th November 1910. It was then brought in parts to the Downs, re-assembled and made a test flight on the 11th November 1910, piloted by Mr. Macdonald. Further flights were made by the following pilots:-Mr. Hammond: Mr. M. Tetard. An aircraft, piloted by Mr. Tetard is reputed to have been the first to fly under the Suspension Bridge. Postcard published by Harvey Barton & Son.

161. B.C. Hucks at Bristol. A card showing one of the many flights which Hucks made on 11th April, 1914, from Buffalo Bill's, or Cody's field. This is now the Memorial Ground, the home of the Bristol Football Club. The houses in the background are in Ellicott and Alton Roads.

162. Bristol Dolphin Swimming Club, pictured on a card postally used in May 1930. Message on the back indicates that Mr. Webber is bringing a strong 2nd team to swim against Mr. Collins' team at Weston-super-Mare. Card published by Savage & White of Thomas St. Bristol.

163. On 10th June 1921, the Prince of Wales came to Bristol to receive the Freedom of the City at the Colston Hall. Later in the afternoon, he visited Fry's Athletic ground (now Phoenix County Ground), to meet the Gloucestershire and Australian cricket teams. The very tall cricketer standing behind the Prince, is W.W. Armstrong, captain of the Australians.

Copyright. **BRISTOL RUGBY FOOTBALL TEAM—Season 1904-5.**

BENNETT(Trnr.) H. WELLINGTON(Sec.) PAUL CHICHESTER VINNICOMBE NEADS DAVIS J.W. JARMAN(Chairman) G. E. LOCKEY
WATSON MOORE THOMAS SMITH(Vice-Capt.) WEBB(Capt.) LAMOND SHEWRING MEYER (Treas.)
WOOD OATEN SPOORS OATES

164. Bristol Rugby Football team. The Bristol Rugby club was formed in 1888 by the joining together of two local clubs, Carlton and Redland Park. Their actual title is Bristol Football Club, with no mention of rugby. Games were played at the Fry's Athletic ground until 1921 season, when the Memorial Ground, Filton Avenue was completed and opened with a match against Cardiff on the 14th September, 1921. Jarman, Moore and Shewring were English Internationals, and Lamond was a Scottish International. Jarman was Bristol's first international player in 1900. The card was published by Art Printers of Bristol.

FIRES

165. Kings Square. This was laid out about the 18th century, with very elegant houses. However, over the years, light industry crept into one or two of the buildings, notably the making of boots and shoes. This card, which was postally used in October 1905, shows the fire at Howard Carr & Co, Boot Factors.

166. Colston Avenue. John Wrights, the printers, were most affected by this fire. Crowds are drawn to the spectacle. Zed Alley would be on the extreme left of the picture, and a wonderful work of art, a Victorian convenience is just visible on the left! The card was postally used in November 1905.

167. Stokes Croft, Derham Boot factory fire, 27th March, 1906. The premises fronted onto Barton Street, Stokes Croft, and were well alight by the time the fire service arrived. The houses opposite caught fire, and the occupants escaped with only the clothes they were wearing. The whole of Derhams, two houses either side, and all the houses opposite were destroyed. Part of the facade of the factory collapsed, burying five firemen, one of whom, Arthur Wale, was killed. Office development now covers this site. Senior & Co. postcard.

168. This tobacconists' kiosk was run by A. E. Bateman on the corner of Milk Street and Old King Street, approximately where Etams dress shop now is. Ridleys Almshouses behind were pulled down in 1913. Earlier the kiosk was used as a watchman's hut (see illus. 22 Vol.2). We see that Ogden's cigarettes cost 5 for a 1d, and the Daily Press of Friday May 10th, 1907 states *"The Colonial Premier's visit to Bristol arranged"* (see illus. 66).

169. J. Glover, grocer of 115, Kingsland Road, St. Phillips. They owned several shops in the St. Phillips area, in Onion Road 1890, Kingsland Road 1902-1914 and Seymour Road, Stapleton Road 1924-34. Prize medal bacon hanging in the doorway! Some of the brand names have disappeared, like Nectar tea and Old Calabar, but Camp coffee and H.P. sauce are still with us.

170. Parry's, the tobacconists of 45 High Street, 1909. What a wonderful display in the window: everything from walking sticks to pipes, cigars, tobacco etc. Presumably the Gentleman with the watch-chain showing is the owner. Note the gas lamp in the door-way.

FUNERALS

171. The funeral procession of James Wright, the son-in-law of George Muller, who founded the Muller's Orphanage in 1836 in Wilson Street, St. Pauls and later at Ashley Down. The procession is passing through what is now the Centre gardens. Art Printers Ltd. postcard, postally used in December 1905.

FUNERAL OF THE LATE MR. JAMES WRIGHT, OF MULLERS ORPHANAGE. Feb. 2nd, 1905.

172. The Procession of the late Joseph Stores Fry, founder of the Fry's chocolate firm on 12th July, 1913, passing along Upper Maudlin Street, now the area of the Bristol Royal Infirmary extension. As can be seen by the long procession of carriages, Joseph Fry was a very important and well-respected man.

173. The funeral of Pte. Bowen passing along Victoria Street. Lovely Byzantine-style building on the right of the picture, now sadly all demolished for the building of Temple Way. The tall chimney in the distance belongs to Fry's chocolate factory in the City.

174. A fancy dress football match organised by the people of the parish of St. Annes, Brislington to raise funds for a parish hall. This was built and opened in June 1921. Among the people in the picture are:-Rev. H.S. Urch, Vicar, Bob Rockett, Bert Atkins and Bert Ford. Can readers identify any others? Photo by G. Thorne.

175. A group of ladies and children in national and gypsy costumes at the Bristol Rovers' Carnival in 1913. Photo by Hamilton of Staple Hill.

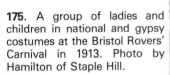

176. A charity football match, possibly at Ashton Gate, on 8th March, 1905. Miss Lily Hawthorne starts the proceedings with the first kick. Postally used in 1906 and published by Ozograph Co. Ltd, St. Michael's Hill, Bristol.

SUFFRAGETTES

177. Suffragette parade leaving Temple Meads station, with many carriages and banners, in the great 1911 demonstration. This, and the next four cards, were published by A.E. Smith of College Green.

178. Marching along Baldwin Street, passing the wholesale fruit and vegetable market. Banners show support from Finland and America.

179. Leaving the Centre and walking toward College Green. It appears to be a Sunday meeting, as the shops are closed and many men have joined the parade. Banners of support from Australia and New Zealand.

180. Leaving College Green to tackle the climb up Park Street. The lady in white is still at the head of the procession.

181. Park Street. It appears to be a very wet and windy day, with coats and banners being blown in the blustery conditions.

"BRISTOL 'VARSITY STUDENTS REVENGE'. THE WRECKED SUFFRAGETTES HEADQUARTERS.

182. The Park Street headquarters of the Suffragette movement was wrecked by University students, in retaliation for the burning down of their sports pavilion at Coombe Dingle by the Suffragettes in 1913.

183. The card was drawn by W.S. Boyd and published by L. Smith of Birmingham. A man about town with a dejected looking dog. Posted at Bristol in November 1906.

184. Postally used in 1912, and published by Wildt & Kray of London. The message on the back reads, *"So sorry to leave Bristol when you are enjoying yourself!"*.

185. Fry's chocolate advert card from the celebrated "Famous Advertisement" series: the artist is Tom Browne, and the card posted in December 1904.

LOCAL POSTCARD PUBLISHERS

Most of the publishers of Bristol postcards were small firms or sub-postmasters, catering for a very limited demand. Only a few, for example E.W. Savory, Charles Worcester, and Harvey Barton, published material of non-local interest. Much research needs to be done on most of these concerns to determine the scope of their output, and the compilers would be pleased to receive any further information about them, and indeed about any hitherto undiscovered postcard publishers. An * indicates that cards by a particular publisher feature in the book.

* A.A. Adams, Oldland Common Post Office
* Art Printers Ltd.
J. Baker & Son, The Mall, Clifton
R. Barnett, North Street
* Harvey Barton & Son Ltd. (H.B.& S.)
J.A. Bickle, Whiteladies Gate
Blyth
W. Brisley, Park Street
Brown & Lloyd, Portland Place, Clifton
S. Burgess, Post Office, Hanham
Burgess & Bown
*Burgess & Co., "Bee" series
*Burleigh Ltd.
Castle-Stationery Co.
Chappell & Co., Redcliffe Printing Works
M.L. Chubb, Shirehampton Post Office
E. Coe, St. Annes Post Office
A.E. Comer, Brislington
F.O. Coward, Bedminster
"Dodson" series
H. Edbrooke, Clifton
L.T. Elson, Brislington & Bristol
A. Emery, Post Office, Patchway
Etches & Co.
H. Evans, Hotwells Road
A.W. Ford
*J.S. Fry & Son
*W. Garratt, 9 Station Road, Ashley Down
A.E. Giddings, Abbots Leigh Post Office
E.J. Giddings, Mangotsfield
Gray & Farr, 35 Abbotsford Road, Redland
H.S. Griffin, 3 Highbury Parade, Bristol
Guillon & Son, Fishponds
J.A. Hamilton, Staple Hill
*Hardings, "Progress" series
*Haywards, 1 Corn Street & 49 High Street
*Hepworth, 66 Church Road, Horfield
W. Hepworth, 366 Gloucester Road
W.M. Hill, 19 Chelsea Park
Henry Hodder & Co. Ltd., Pioneer Cash
    Chemists
A. Hodgson, 64 Victoria Street
E.C. Hollister, Sandy Park Post Office
A.E. Hornsey, Bedminster Parade
Horton
J.B. & S.C., "Avonvale" series
Kelly & Harvey, Gloucester Road
* Fred Little (reproduction of Victorian photographs)

Wilfrid Loft, 323 Wells Road, Knowle
S. Loxton, 7 St. Augustin's Parade
W.F. Mack, 52 Park Row
A.H.N. Middleton
Mitchell & Co., 30 Baldwin Street
"Ozograph" series, 145 St. Michaels Hill
D.G. Parker, 4 Birchwood Road, St. Annes
    Park
E.S. Pearce, Post Office Shirehampton
Pincock Bros.
Plucknett, Kingswood
*E. Pomeroy, Longwell Green
M.J.R.
Rising, 156 Whiteladies Road, Clifton
A.G. Roberts, Eastville
S.E. Robinson, Shirehampton Post Office
A.F.S.
*C.S. & Co.
*L.S., Fishponds
*Savage & White, 114 Thomas St.
E.W. Savory & Co.
Scholastic Trading Co.
*Senior & Co., Cotham Hill
J.T. Shapland
*A.G. Short & Co., "Chatterton" series
*F.C. Sincock, The Library, Westbury-on-
    Trym
*A.E. Smith, 44 College Green
F. Snary, 26 Castle Street
W.A.W. Sprod, 101 Stokes Croft
T. Stanley, East Street, Bedminster
E.C. Stevens, 12 Arley Hill
W. Stevenson, Bruton Place, Clifton
Stevinson, "C" series
F.W. Taylor, Clifton
S.J. Thomas, Boyces Avenue, Clifton
Veale and Co., Bristol
*Viner and Co., Bath and Weston-super-
    Mare
West Counties Agency, 14 Westfield Park,
    Redland
Wickhams Ltd
Winchester
Stanley Wood, Sea Mills Post Office
Charles Worcester & Co.
Wyman & Sons Ltd.
York Publishing Co.
*"York" series, 11 Lower Maudlin Street
J.C. Young, Redfield

BRISTOL POSTCARD CLUB

THE CLUB'S first meeting took place at the Swan Hotel in November 1981, with an attendance of forty. After a successful first year, an exhibition and fair was held in November 1982, mainly to publicise the club. An entry to the competition at the British International Postcard Exhibition (September 1983) secured first prize in the club section. Members also supply cards to the *Bristol Evening Post* for their "Changing Face of Bristol" series, and cards have been exhibited in local libraries and building society offices. In June 1984, the club's move to new premises - in the Common Room of St. Stephen's Church - proved very popular with members as it is more central. Meetings are held on the first Monday of each month, starting at 7.30 p.m.

Details can be obtained from secretary Gladys Lawes, 84 High Street, Portishead, Bristol BS20 9AJ.